BARNIE'S COFFEE & TEA COMPANY®

The Coffee & Tea Lover's Cookbook

Oxmoor House®

Library of Congress Catalog Card Number: 95-68922
ISBN: 0-8487-1490-3
Manufactured in the United States of America
First Printing 1995

Barnie's Coffee & Tea Company® Staff Contributors
    President: Barnie Philip Jones
    Vice President, Marketing & Purchasing: Jamie Utendorf
    Supervisor, Marketing: Pamela Starr
    Coordinator, Promotions: Kelly Smith
    Coffee Buyer: Robert Carpenter
    Sous Chef: David Woolley
    Mallard Design Group: Shipman Mallard

Oxmoor House, Inc.
  Editor-in-Chief: Nancy Fitzpatrick Wyatt
  Senior Foods Editor: Susan Carlisle Payne
  Senior Editor, Editorial Services: Olivia Kindig Wells
  Art Director: James Boone

The Coffee & Tea Lover's Cookbook
  Editor: Julie Fisher
  Designers: Alison Turner Bachofer, Elizabeth Passey Edge
  Copy Editors: Holly Ensor, Jacqueline Giovanelli
  Editorial Assistant: Stacey Geary
  Director, Test Kitchens: Kathleen Royal Phillips
  Assistant Director, Test Kitchens: Gayle Hays Sadler
  Test Kitchen Home Economists: Susan Hall Bellows,
    Julie Christopher, Iris Crawley, Michele Brown Fuller,
    Natalie E. King, Elizabeth Tyler Luckett, Jan A. Smith
  Senior Photographer: Jim Bathie
  Senior Photo Stylist: Kay E. Clarke
  Contributing Photo Stylists: Virginia R. Cravens, Cathy Muir, Angie N. Sinclair
  Publishing Systems Administrator: Rick Tucker
  Production and Distribution Director: Phillip Lee
  Production Manager: Gail Morris
  Associate Production Manager: Theresa L. Beste
  Production Assistant: Marianne Jordan
  Project Manager: Teresa Wilson Lux

Cover: *Caramel-Brownie Cheesecake (page 65), Caramel Nut Mocha (page 92)*

Call 1-800-284-1416 to order Barnie's coffees, teas, and gifts.

CONTENTS

FOREWORD

One of life's greatest pleasures is the universal pastime of drinking a cup of coffee—whether at home in the morning, at the office during a coffee break, or at the end of a fine meal. This enjoyable experience represents the fruits of the labor of millions of people involved in the coffee industry around the globe. A moment of sipping coffee is the culmination of fourteen centuries of innovation.

For me, the quest for the perfect cup of coffee began in graduate school in the late 1970s when I was staying up late at night writing my dissertation. I had never been much of a coffee drinker until those midnight studying binges. The "stuff"—I hesitate to call it coffee—purchased from the grocery store bothered my stomach. Fortunately, I happened upon a quaint coffee shop selling arabica coffees from around the world. These specialty coffees had spicy aromas, great tastes, and exotic names. My poor stomach loved them!

Little by little, I became a coffee drinker and a coffee connoisseur. Later, I finished grad school and decided it could be enjoyable to share my coffee discovery with friends. In 1980, in my hometown of Orlando, Florida, I opened the first Barnie's Coffee & Tea Company®. It was a small shop that specialized in high quality arabica coffees. At Barnie's, we didn't just sell coffee, we loved coffee! We also valued the friends and customers who frequented the shop. It became our mission to introduce these good people to our passion for specialty coffee. The same zeal for our coffee still can be felt in the many Barnie's stores throughout the United States and seen in our employees' faces. Each Barnie's establishment has a deep sense of pride and joy in sharing our fine coffees.

Over the years, I have had the opportunity to travel the world and meet people involved in the coffee industry. As a past president of the Specialty Coffee Association of America®, I have been privileged to develop lasting friendships with fellow coffee lovers in such coffee-producing nations as Costa Rica, Brazil, Colombia, Guatemala, Kenya, Ethiopia, Indonesia, and the United States (including Hawaii). I have also come to appreciate the unique social customs that accompany coffee consumption not only all over the United States and Canada but also in Japan, Germany, Norway, and Italy.

At Barnie's, our love of coffee has made all of us coffee perfectionists. We are on a never-ending journey to find the finest coffees in the world to share with our friends and customers. I hope our book will invigorate your epicurean interest in this extraordinary brewed bean. May you become a coffee lover and perfectionist yourself. Enjoy!

Barnie Philip Jones

BARNIE PHILIP JONES
Founder & President
Barnie's Coffee & Tea Company®

COFFEE TALK

$\mathcal{W}$hen you hold a cup of steaming aromatic coffee in your hands, you hold one of the world's most cherished beverages. With centuries of legend behind it, the coffee process from seed to cup is an achievement— the culmination of the experience, skill, and handiwork of hundreds of individuals.

Whether you're a novice to the brew or a coffee connoisseur, you can appreciate the labor of love that goes into every cup. About 50 handpicked beans are in each cup you drink. And there are more than 2,000 beans in every pound of coffee—a full year's production of one coffee tree!

Coffee falls into two basic categories. The first is *coffea robusta*, a workaday-type coffee that can be compared to a jug wine. The second is *coffea arabica*, the "aristocrat" of coffee, the best of which is comparable to fine estate wines. The specialty arabicas at Barnie's meet standards beyond even the best gourmet coffees. They're selected from only the very best arabica trees from the most renowned coffee estates in the world.

HOW COFFEE IS GROWN

Coffee is grown throughout Africa, the Americas, Asia, and the South Pacific, areas where the right combination of temperature, rain, sunshine, altitude, and rich volcanic soil is present.

Specialty arabica coffee grows best at altitudes of 3,300 to 7,000 feet. Coffee trees on plantations are generally pruned to six feet tall and are organized in rows that are four to nine feet apart.

A coffee tree begins flowering in its third year. White flowers bloom in clusters at the

A coffee tree branch with ripe red cherries

Green Bean
(unroasted)

Pulp

Cherry

*The coffee bean
within the cherry*

*Roasted
coffee bean*

THE HARVESTING OF COFFEE

Specialty arabica coffee cherries grow for six to seven months—two months longer than their lowland robusta cousins. The harvesting of a crop of cherries is an ongoing, tedious task. Only the ripe cherries can be picked. And since coffee cherries do not ripen all at the same time, each tree must be carefully handpicked and revisited several times during the harvest.

In most coffee-producing countries when it is time to harvest, everyone picks—friends, family, and neighbors. Pickers usually use ladders to reach the highest branches and use a basket called a *canasta* (above left) which is attached to the picker's waist so both hands are free to pick. After the coffee cherries are harvested, they're sifted to remove twigs, leaves, and small stones (below).

base of the leaves. The flowers bloom for only three to four days; then the fruit, called cherries, begins to develop in clusters at the base of each leaf. The cherries start out hard and green, but ripen to be plump and bright red and, in a few species, yellow. A coffee tree generally produces its first good crop in its fifth to sixth year.

Like grapes used in producing fine wine, coffee beans develop their own unique qualities and characteristics that are never quite the same from year to year, harvest to harvest. At Barnie's, we recognize that uniqueness, and this is why our search is endless for coffees that embody the very finest characteristics.

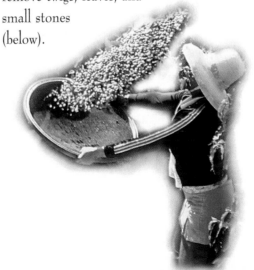

THE PROCESSING OF COFFEE

Once coffee cherries are picked, there are two methods of processing the coffee. The dry method is the oldest and most natural process, in which the coffee cherries collected are immediately spread out to dry on patios in the sun. However, most specialty coffees are processed by a second method called the wet process or "washed." In this process, coffee cherries are collected and placed in receiving tanks filled with water. Leaves, sticks, and inferior cherries are separated from the ripe cherries, which sink to the bottom.

Drying coffee on patios in Costa Rica

Next, it is critical to gently separate the cherry pulp from the sticky green bean inside. The pulping machines are designed to use water and pressure to actually squeeze the bean from the ripe cherry. The beans are then placed in large tanks and allowed to ferment for 12 to 24 hours.

Fermentation allows naturally occurring enzymes to remove the sticky residue called *mucilage* that covers the beans. Once the beans are thoroughly washed and all of the sticky mucilage is removed, the beans are then drained of their water.

THE DRYING OF COFFEE

After specialty coffee beans are drained, they are at a moisture level of 65% and need to be dried to a moisture level of 12%. This is done in three different ways.

First, the traditional way of drying coffee is on concrete patios in the sun. This process requires constant raking and turning of the beans for three to ten days, depending on the weather.

Because it takes so long to sun-dry coffee beans, and because drying is necessary in areas where the rain is constant during harvesting, a second method of drying is used. Large drum dryers with indirect heat

Roasting beans in a sample roaster

water content, bean density (hardness), and overall appearance.

THE SECRET OF ROASTING COFFEE

While much skill and labor have gone into the coffee during the growing, harvesting, processing, and drying stages, the green bean yet awaits the art of roasting to bring out its true nature and full potential.

Each variety of specialty coffee has its own unique flavor characteristics. Decisions about how quickly to roast, and how dark to roast are factors that affect these characteristics and the eventual cup of coffee.

At Barnie's, we roast each of our coffees to its peak level, thus achieving that fine balance in which the distinguishing varietal characteristics are most pronounced. While pale coffees found in grocery stores have given rise to the popular belief that dark roasting is best, we know each variety of coffee deserves unique treatment.

Dark roasting actually destroys the more delicate flavor and subtle aromatics that distinguish coffees of one region from another. It can also disguise the deficiencies of a lesser quality bean since dark roasting actually "burns" the bean, making the dominant flavor the resulting carbon instead of the varietal character.

gently revolve and dry the coffee beans from the inside out.

Today, most small processors on plantations use a third method of drying which combines sun-drying with drying in the gently heated, revolving drum dryers. The dried coffee beans are then milled to remove their parchment, a natural protective husk. After the parchment is removed, the beans are graded and divided according to size,

BREWING THE PERFECT CUP

The final step in achieving the perfect cup of coffee is in your hands. The first rule of making perfect coffee is to buy freshly roasted beans and to guard that freshness until the moment you pour it into your cup. This is essential because once coffee is roasted, it begins to lose its freshness. The best way to store coffee is in an airtight container in the refrigerator. Whole beans retain flavor longer than ground coffee, so buy whole beans in small quantities that will be used within a week or two, and grind only what you will need for each pot.

Home grinders come in two varieties—electric blade grinders and burr grinders. The blade grinder, a cost-effective way of grinding coffee at home, is controlled by hand and timed by you to determine the grind best suited for your particular taste and coffee maker. Burr grinders are higher priced. They compress two blades together and actually pulverize the beans. This method creates a more even grind that exposes more of the fine coffee flavor and oils to the brewing water. Usually this type of grinder allows you to select the fineness of the grind and the number of cups you want.

Choosing the fineness of the grind is truly a matter of taste. Use the following chart as a starting point; then adjust the grind to your own preference.

How Fine To Grind

Coarse: French press pots, percolators, or Toddy®

Medium: Basket-drip coffee makers

Fine: Cone-drip coffee makers

Espresso: Extra fine for espresso machines

Turkish: Pulverized fine powder for Turkish ibriks

Selecting a coffee maker is the next critical step, and there are several styles from which to choose.

Non-Electric Coffee Makers

The Melitta®-style and Chemex®-style pour-through coffee makers are the most noteworthy for use with specialty coffee. Both use a cone-shaped filter for holding the coffee grounds. Water that is almost boiling is poured over the grounds, and hot coffee seeps through the filter into a reservoir.

Another style is the French press coffee maker, which has enjoyed recent popularity for its classic design and ability to produce a rich, clean coffee. Similar in concept to a teapot, ground coffee is put into the bottom of the pot, and water that is almost boiling is poured over it. The coffee floats to the top of the pot and is allowed to steep. After a few minutes, a filter plunger is used to force the grounds to the bottom of the pot.

The Toddy® cold water coffee maker is a unique device that eliminates most of the acidity found in coffee, making the resulting brew much gentler on sensitive stomachs. To use the Toddy coffee maker, simply place a pound of ground coffee into the filter, fill top container with cold water, and allow to steep for 24 hours. Then pull out the filter and allow the concentrate to strain into a carafe.

Toddy coffee concentrate is ideal for creating iced coffee drinks as well as hot coffee beverages.

Electric Drip Coffee Makers

When choosing an electric drip coffee maker, look for these specific features. First, the coffee maker should have a cone-shaped filter basket rather than a flat basket. A gold-mesh filter is best for the environment, and a 23-karat gold-mesh filter won't absorb the coffee's flavorful oils the way paper filters do.

The coffee maker should heat the water to between 200° and 205°, and then hold the coffee on a warmer at 185° to 190°. Coffee that is brewed and allowed to sit on a hot plate deteriorates quickly. A good rule of thumb is to never keep coffee on a burner for longer than 15 minutes.

The best appliances brew coffee right into a thermal carafe. Keeping fresh-brewed coffee in a thermal carafe is preferred because it locks in flavor and aroma. If your coffee maker does not offer this feature, purchase a thermal carafe in which to keep brewed coffee fresh and hot.

COFFEE COMPANIONS

*W*hen developing a menu, the coffee choice should be given as much thought as a good wine selection. Here are some suggestions for pairing compatible coffees and foods.

Classically Simple

These coffees offer the classic simplicity of a clean, mild cup with a natural sweetness. Enjoy them with light fruits and pastries, Chinese and Japanese cuisines, fish, delicate breakfast pastries, and desserts.

Brazilian Mocha Lavado
light body, soft cup
Hawaiian Kona
light body, mellow, sweet
Barnie's Special Blend
medium body, mellow, aromatic
Barnie's Blend™
full body, mellow, sweet
Java Estate
full body, mellow, creamy

(Ripe coffee cherries shown at left)

Legendary Masterpieces

You'll find a masterful balance of bright acidity, exotic flavors, full body, and fragrant cup in these coffees. Foods that fare well with these coffees are traditional breakfast or brunch foods, steaks, barbecue, sandwiches, French cuisine, ice cream, cakes, fruit cobblers, tarts, and pies.

Papua New Guinea
full body, mild, sweet
Barnie's Rare Blend
full body, mellow, rich and smooth
Guatemala Antigua
full body, exotic, fragrant
Mocha Java
full body, mild, aromatic
Colombian Bucaramanga
full body, mild, mellow
Costa Rican Tres Rios
full body, tangy, exotic
Kenya AA
full body, winy, rich
Tanzanian Peaberry
medium body, tangy, clean and bright

Commanding Performances

These coffees have an intense, full flavor and a rich, bold taste. Foods that can hold up to these full flavors are French pastries, spicy Mexican fare, hardy Italian pastas, and rich desserts.

Ethiopian Yrgacheffe
medium body, spicy, sweet
Puerto Rican Yauco Selecto
full body, rich, chocolaty
Sumatra Mandheling
heavy body, earthy, intense
Barnie's Premium Blend
full body, tangy, aromatic
French Roast
heavy body, syrupy, bold
Golden Espresso Blend™
full body, spicy, soft and clean finish
Espresso Roast
full body, rich and sweet

As more coffee lovers develop a trained palate for specialty coffee, more are selecting flavored coffees, as well, for variety and the fun of savoring different coffee nuances.

Instrumental Beginnings

These flavored coffees are great breakfast or brunch companions. Try them with your favorite recipes from the "Awakenings" chapter that begins on page 17.

Coffee Cake®
Cinnamon Butter Cookie
Chocolate Macadamia Nut
Cinnamon 'n' Spice

Harmonious Endings

These coffees are excellent dessert partners after lunch or dinner. Enjoy them with the "Scrumptious Endings" desserts beginning on page 59.

German Chocolate Cake®
Cookies 'n' Cream
Bananas Foster
Amaretto
Vanilla Cream

Captivating Finales

At only 8 calories per cup and 0 grams of fat, flavored coffees are a delicious dessert alternative.

Decadent Dark Chocolate
White Chocolate Mousse
Spiced Butter Rum
Tiramisu
Hazelnut
Santa's White Christmas™
Traditional Holiday Blend™
Irish Cream

To enjoy these coffee selections and more, call 1-800-284-1416.

Tea Time

Ancient Origins

The origins of tea are shrouded in ancient lore and tradition. It's thought that the first people to enjoy the pleasures of tea were in Southeast Asia. Through the centuries, tea has been a passion of many people and cultures. The Chinese and Japanese are famous for their delicate tea ceremonies, and the English are well-known for believing that a nice cup of tea could help solve almost any problem.

At different points in history, tea has been used as currency, medicine, stimulant, and refreshment. It has been prepared in cakes, whipped in water, and even flavored with onion! Today, tea is most often enjoyed steeped and served either steaming hot or poured over ice.

A Flavorful Harvest

Like specialty coffee, tea varieties are determined by where they are grown and how they are handled. The finest teas grow at high altitudes—5,000 feet or above—and where there is at least 100 inches of rainfall a year. To ensure the most flavorful leaves, these tea plants are kept pruned to about three feet, and only the new, tiny, delicate shoots and buds are harvested by hand. The "first flush" or "fine pluck" are the youngest, most tender leaves and buds, which result in the finest tasting tea.

Tea Types

Tea enjoyed today is one of three types: green, black, or oolong. They all come from the same plant, but are processed differently. For all three types of tea, quality depends on the condition of the actual tea leaves when they reach the processing facility. For the finest tea, the leaves must be all the same size, fresh, unbruised, and free from extra materials such as twigs. This results in even drying and fermenting.

Green tea is dried, but not fermented. Tea leaves are steamed, and then rolled to bruise the leaves and release the tea's characteristic flavor. They are then dried with hot, dry air. Also known as "firing," drying is alternated with rolling until the leaves are crisp and twisted. When steeped, the taste of green tea most closely resembles that of a fresh tea leaf.

> *Two of the most popular types of green tea are Gunpowder and Panfired.*

Black tea is created when the leaves are allowed to ferment. Fermentation happens when the tea leaves' juices (squeezed out by rolling) are allowed to mix with oxygen before drying. This changes the color and flavor of the tea, making it dark and mellow.

> *Favorite black teas include Ceylon Broken Orange Pekoe, Earl Grey, and Gold-Tipped Darjeeling.*

Oolong tea is semi-fermented. The process is similar to that of black tea, but the fermentation process is much shorter. This results in a tea which has characteristics of both green and black tea.

> *Formosa Oolong is perhaps the most well-known oolong tea.*

Flavored tea is black tea with herbs, bits of fruit, spices, nuts, or other types of flavorings added. These teas range from the traditional (honey) to the exotic (Piña Colada). Most flavored teas can be enjoyed hot, but are especially delicious when prepared as iced tea. Their refreshing flavors are a treat for any time of the day.

Preparing the Perfect Cup

Traditional tea is easy to make; it just requires a few careful steps. Fill a kettle with fresh, cold water, and bring it to a rolling boil. Meanwhile, fill a teapot with hot water to warm it. This will encourage the leaves to open properly. Place 1 teaspoon (per 6-ounce cup) of your favorite loose tea into an infuser, or allow one tea bag per cup. When making six or more cups, add one extra teaspoon (or tea bag) for the pot. Empty the pre-warmed teapot, add tea, and pour in the boiling water. Allow the tea to steep for three to five minutes for black teas and five to ten minutes for green or herbal teas. Then pour and enjoy!

Iced tea is usually made by pouring hot tea over ice. However, increase the strength to 1½ teaspoons per 6 ounces of water (or three tea bags for every 12 ounces of water). The extra tea is necessary to counter the effect of ice diluting the tea.

Iced tea can also be made with a cold-water process. Simply add cold water to the tea leaves or bags; cover and let stand for six to nine hours. Stir or gently shake the container every few hours. Strain the tea or remove the tea bags to enjoy. This process is sometimes referred to as "sun tea" and creates a delicious iced tea that is not bitter!

Tea Concentrate

For extra convenience, tea concentrate can be used to make hot or iced tea. The liquid concentrate is steeped in cold water to ensure a taste that is smooth and acid-free.

To prepare perfect tea, combine 1 part concentrate with 7 parts fresh hot or cold water; then add sugar, lemon, or milk. The concentrate can be used to quickly make delicious tea by the glass or by the pitcher!

Tea on Occasion

Here are two fresh ideas for showcasing tea among friends, family, and coworkers.

A Blushing Bridal Tea

Choose a garden setting, serve light refreshments, and don the bride's table with your finest delicate accessories—including a silver tea service and crisp white linens.

Serve light or fruit-flavored teas such as Gold-Tipped Darjeeling, French Vanilla, Strawberries 'n' Cream, Passion Fruit, or China Rose. Garnish an assortment of dainty tea cups with thin lemon slices or edible flower petals. Use a favorite antique teapot as a centerpiece base for flowers. Tie napkins and silverware with ivy, and attach additional edible flowers at each place setting. Remember, tradition calls for tea to be poured by close friends, so have a member of the wedding party do the honors.

A Professional Power Tea

This executive function is a great idea for meetings with clients, or it can be a tea "happy hour" with friends right after work.

Serve bold and brisk teas such as a selection of Assam, English Breakfast, Irish Blend, or Ceylon teas. These choices hold their flavor well. Offer milk, sugar, and lemon as accompaniments. This is not meant to be a dainty affair; you can prepare tea in advance, keep it warm, and serve it from a thermal carafe. Bone china or sturdy office mugs are appropriate.

For morning meetings, serve quiche, sliced fruit, bagels, or scones. For afternoon sessions, serve crackers and cheese, finger sandwiches, cheese wafers, and spiced nuts.

Awakenings

Mocha

Pancakes

1 cup all-purpose flour

2 teaspoons baking powder

½ teaspoon salt

3 tablespoons sugar

2 teaspoons finely ground espresso beans

1 large egg

¾ cup milk

2 tablespoons butter or margarine, melted

1 (1-ounce) square semisweet chocolate, melted

Combine first 5 ingredients in a large bowl; make a well in center of mixture. Combine egg and remaining ingredients, stirring well. Add to dry ingredients, stirring just until dry ingredients are moistened.

Pour about ¼ cup batter for each pancake onto a hot, lightly greased griddle or skillet. Cook pancakes until tops are covered with bubbles and edges look cooked; turn and cook other side. Serve with maple syrup or chocolate syrup. Yield: 12 (4-inch) pancakes.

For a dazzling dessert option, top Mocha Pancakes with a scoop of vanilla ice cream and hot fudge topping.

(Photograph of Mocha Pancakes on preceding page)

Maple
French Toast Casserole

Place bread cubes in a lightly greased 13- x 9- x 2-inch baking dish, and set aside.

Beat cream cheese at medium speed of an electric mixer until smooth; add eggs and remaining ingredients, beating until blended. Pour over bread cubes; cover and refrigerate 8 hours or overnight.

Remove from refrigerator; let stand at room temperature 30 minutes. Bake at 375° for 40 to 50 minutes or until set, covering with foil after 25 minutes. Serve with additional syrup. Yield: 12 servings.

Sip Barnie's Cinnamon 'n' Spice Coffee along with this maple-flavored French toast. For variety, you can substitute cinnamon-raisin bread for white sandwich bread.

◆

16 slices white sandwich bread, cut into 1-inch cubes

1 (8-ounce) package cream cheese, softened

12 large eggs

2 cups whipping cream

½ cup maple syrup

½ teaspoon maple flavoring

◆

Raspberry-Almond
Biscuits

Combine first 5 ingredients in a large bowl; cut in butter with a pastry blender until mixture is crumbly. Stir in almonds and orange rind. Add milk and yogurt, stirring with a fork until dry ingredients are moistened. (Dough will be very sticky.)

Add raspberries, stirring gently. Turn dough out onto a heavily floured surface, and knead lightly 5 or 6 times.

Roll dough to ¾-inch thickness; cut with a 2¼-inch round cutter. Place biscuits on a lightly greased baking sheet. Bake at 425° for 15 minutes or until lightly browned. Yield: 20 biscuits.

Enjoy the subtle berry flavor of Barnie's Raspberries 'n' Cream® Tea while savoring these buttery biscuits plumped with fruit.

3 cups all-purpose flour

1 tablespoon baking powder

½ teaspoon baking soda

⅛ teaspoon salt

½ cup sugar

¾ cup butter or margarine, cut into pieces

½ cup chopped almonds

1½ teaspoons grated orange rind

¾ cup milk

¾ cup plain yogurt

1 cup fresh or frozen raspberries, thawed and well drained

Cinnamon-Raisin

Breakfast Biscuits

1⅓ cups corn flakes cereal

2 tablespoons brown sugar

1 teaspoon ground cinnamon

2 tablespoons butter or margarine, melted

2½ cups biscuit and baking mix

2 tablespoons sugar

½ cup raisins

⅓ cup buttermilk

⅓ cup tonic water

½ teaspoon vanilla extract

Sour Cream Frosting (facing page)

Combine first 3 ingredients in container of an electric blender or food processor; cover and process until mixture resembles fine crumbs. Transfer to a small bowl; add butter, stirring until dry ingredients are moistened. Set aside.

Combine biscuit mix, sugar, and raisins in a large bowl; add buttermilk, tonic water, and vanilla, stirring with a fork just until dry ingredients are moistened.

Turn dough out onto a lightly floured surface, and knead lightly 3 or 4 times. Gradually sprinkle with crumb mixture, kneading just until crumb mixture is blended into dough.

Shape into 12 balls, and place on a lightly greased baking sheet. Press each into a ½-inch-thick biscuit.

Bake at 400° for 15 to 18 minutes or until browned. Transfer immediately to a wire rack, and spread with Sour Cream Frosting. Yield: 1 dozen.

Sour Cream Frosting

Combine powdered sugar, butter, sour cream, and vanilla in a small bowl. Stir until blended. Yield: ⅔ cup.

1½ cups sifted powdered sugar

2 tablespoons butter or margarine, melted

2 tablespoons sour cream

1 teaspoon vanilla extract

Rise 'n' Shine

Biscuits

Combine first 3 ingredients in a medium bowl; add biscuit mix, stirring with a fork just until dry ingredients are moistened. Turn dough out onto a lightly floured surface, and knead lightly 10 to 12 times.

Roll dough to 1-inch thickness; cut with a 2¼-inch round cutter. Place 1 biscuit in the center of a lightly greased 8-inch round cakepan; arrange remaining biscuits around center biscuit. Bake at 425° for 12 to 14 minutes or until golden. Yield: 6 biscuits.

⅓ cup club soda

⅓ cup sour cream

1½ tablespoons sugar

2 cups biscuit and baking mix

Apricot-Almond
Coffee Cake

1 cup butter or margarine, softened

2 cups sugar

2 large eggs

2 cups all-purpose flour

1 teaspoon baking powder

¼ teaspoon salt

1 (8-ounce) carton sour cream

1 teaspoon almond extract

1 cup sliced almonds

1 (10-ounce) jar apricot preserves

Beat butter at medium speed of an electric mixer about 2 minutes or until creamy. Gradually add sugar, beating at medium speed 5 to 7 minutes. Add eggs, one at a time, beating after each addition.

Combine flour, baking powder, and salt; add to butter mixture alternately with sour cream, beginning and ending with flour mixture. Mix at low speed just until blended after each addition. Stir in almond extract.

Spoon about one-third of batter into a greased and floured 12-cup Bundt pan. Sprinkle with half of almonds, and dot with half of apricot preserves. Top with remaining batter; sprinkle with remaining almonds, and dot with remaining preserves.

Bake at 350° for 50 to 55 minutes or until a wooden pick inserted in center comes out clean. Cool in pan on a wire rack 15 minutes; remove from pan, and let cool completely on wire rack. Yield: one 10-inch coffee cake.

Serve Barnie's delicately flavored Apricot Tea or English Breakfast Tea with this tender coffee cake studded with almonds.

Espresso Swirl
Coffee Cake

Combine first 3 ingredients, stirring well. Cut in ¼ cup butter with a pastry blender until mixture resembles coarse crumbs. Set aside.

Beat ½ cup softened butter at medium speed of an electric mixer until creamy; gradually add 1 cup sugar, beating well. Add eggs, one at a time, beating after each addition.

Combine sour cream and baking soda; stir well, and set aside. Combine 2 cups flour, baking powder, and salt; add to egg mixture alternately with sour cream mixture, beginning and ending with flour mixture. Mix at low speed just until blended after each addition. Stir in chocolate morsels.

Pour batter into a buttered 13- x 9- x 2-inch pan. Sprinkle espresso streusel mixture over batter. Swirl batter gently with a knife, if desired.

Bake at 350° for 30 to 35 minutes or until a wooden pick inserted in center comes out clean. Cool in pan on a wire rack. Yield: 12 servings.

Soothing café au lait, typically served in huge coffee bowls, is the ideal accompaniment for this rich breakfast cake.

⧫

⅔ cup firmly packed brown sugar

¼ cup plus 2 tablespoons all-purpose flour

1½ tablespoons finely ground espresso beans

¼ cup unsalted butter

½ cup unsalted butter, softened

1 cup sugar

3 large eggs, lightly beaten

1 cup sour cream

½ teaspoon baking soda

2 cups all-purpose flour

1 teaspoon baking powder

¼ teaspoon salt

1 cup semisweet chocolate morsels

⧫

Barnie's Best
Coffee Cake

1 cup pecan pieces

¾ cup firmly packed brown sugar

¼ cup sugar

1 teaspoon ground cinnamon

½ cup butter or margarine, softened

1 cup sugar

2 large eggs

2 cups all-purpose flour

2 teaspoons baking powder

½ teaspoon baking soda

½ teaspoon salt

1 cup sour cream

1 teaspoon vanilla extract

Combine first 4 ingredients in a small bowl, stirring well.

Beat butter at medium speed of an electric mixer about 2 minutes or until creamy. Gradually add 1 cup sugar, beating at medium speed 5 to 7 minutes. Add eggs, one at a time, beating after each addition.

Combine flour, baking powder, soda, and salt; add to butter mixture alternately with sour cream, beginning and ending with flour mixture. Mix at low speed just until blended after each addition. Stir in vanilla.

Pour half of batter into a lightly greased 13- x 9- x 2-inch pan. Sprinkle half of pecan mixture over batter. Repeat procedure with remaining batter and pecan mixture. Bake at 325° for 40 to 45 minutes. Cool in pan on a wire rack. Yield: 12 servings.

Start your day off right with a cappuccino or a cup of Barnie's Blend™ Coffee and a slice of Barnie's family's favorite coffee cake.

Spiced Blueberry
Kuchen

1 cup all-purpose flour

2 tablespoons sugar

1/8 teaspoon salt

1/8 teaspoon ground
cinnamon

1/2 cup butter or margarine

1 tablespoon white vinegar

5 cups fresh blueberries,
divided

2/3 cup sugar

2 tablespoons all-purpose
flour

1/4 teaspoon ground
cinnamon

Combine first 4 ingredients in a small bowl;
cut in butter with a pastry blender until mixture is crumbly. Sprinkle vinegar over flour
mixture; stir with a fork just until dry ingredients are moistened. Shape into a ball.

Press pastry firmly onto bottom and 1 inch
up sides of an ungreased 9-inch springform
pan. Sprinkle 3 cups blueberries over pastry.
Combine 2/3 cup sugar, 2 tablespoons flour,
and 1/4 teaspoon cinnamon in a small bowl;
stir well. Sprinkle sugar mixture over blueberries in pan.

Bake on lowest rack of oven at 400° for 50
to 60 minutes or until crust is golden. Remove
from oven; top with remaining 2 cups blueberries. Cool in pan on a wire rack. Carefully
remove sides of springform pan. Cut into
wedges to serve. Yield: 8 servings.

*Kuchen is a fruit-filled or cheese-filled cake that originated in Germany but now enjoys many variations
worldwide. Serve this blueberry version for breakfast
with Barnie's Special Blend Coffee.*

Pineapple Ambrosia
Crumble

Combine 1 cup coconut, flour, ⅔ cup sugar, and brown sugar in a medium bowl. Cut in butter with a pastry blender until mixture is crumbly. Set aside.

Combine remaining ½ cup coconut, ¼ cup sugar, pineapple, banana, orange, and pineapple juice in a large bowl; toss gently. Spoon fruit mixture into a buttered 13- x 9- x 2-inch baking dish; sprinkle reserved coconut streusel mixture over fruit.

Bake at 350° for 40 to 45 minutes or until golden. Serve warm. Yield: 12 servings.

Greek mythology claims ambrosia to be the "food of the Gods." This crumb-topped fruit mixture lives up to its name—try it à la mode for dessert!

◆

1½ cups flaked coconut, divided

1 cup all-purpose flour

⅔ cup sugar

½ cup firmly packed brown sugar

½ cup butter or margarine

¼ cup sugar

½ fresh pineapple, cut into 1-inch cubes (3 cups)

3 large bananas, sliced

3 large oranges, peeled and sectioned

2 tablespoons pineapple juice

◆

Nutty
Granola

2½ cups regular oats, uncooked

2½ cups whole wheat flake cereal

1 cup flaked coconut

½ cup wheat germ

½ cup sesame seeds

½ cup sunflower kernels

½ cup dry-roasted peanuts

½ cup butter or margarine

½ cup firmly packed brown sugar

½ cup honey

1 teaspoon vanilla extract

Combine first 7 ingredients in a large bowl; stir well, and set aside.

Combine butter, brown sugar, and honey in a small saucepan. Cook over medium heat, stirring constantly, until butter melts and mixture is thoroughly heated. Remove from heat. Stir in vanilla, and pour over oat mixture, coating evenly.

Spoon into a lightly greased 15- x 10- x 1-inch jellyroll pan. Bake at 275° for 1 hour and 15 minutes or until golden, stirring every 15 minutes. Remove from oven; stir occasionally as mixture cools. Store in an airtight container. Yield: 10 cups.

Linger over a cup of Barnie's Espresso Roast while you munch on this nutty cereal.

Bacon and Cheese
Muffins

Combine first 6 ingredients in a large bowl; make a well in center of mixture. Combine egg, milk, and oil; add to dry ingredients, stirring just until dry ingredients are moistened. Spoon batter into well-greased muffin pans, filling two-thirds full.

Bake at 400° for 20 to 22 minutes or until golden. Remove from pans immediately. Yield: 1 dozen.

1¾ cups all-purpose flour

2½ teaspoons baking powder

½ teaspoon salt

½ cup (2 ounces) shredded sharp Cheddar cheese

2 tablespoons sugar

10 slices bacon, cooked and crumbled

1 large egg, lightly beaten

¾ cup milk

⅓ cup vegetable oil

Banana Nut

Muffins

1¾ cups all-purpose flour

2½ teaspoons baking powder

½ teaspoon salt

½ cup sugar

1 large egg, lightly beaten

¾ cup mashed ripe banana

½ cup milk

⅓ cup vegetable oil

½ cup chopped pecans or hazelnuts

½ cup butterscotch morsels (optional)

Combine first 4 ingredients in a large bowl; make a well in center of mixture.

Combine egg, banana, milk, and oil; add to dry ingredients, stirring just until dry ingredients are moistened. Stir in nuts. Add butterscotch morsels, if desired. Spoon batter into greased muffin pans, filling three-fourths full.

Bake at 400° for 18 to 20 minutes or until golden. Remove from pans immediately. Yield: 1 dozen.

Note: You can also bake the batter for Banana Nut Muffins as a loaf. Spoon batter into a greased 9- x 5- x 3-inch loafpan, and bake at 350° for 45 to 50 minutes. Let cool in pan 10 minutes.

Pour a cup of Barnie's Hazelnut Coffee to complement these muffins that are reminiscent of an old favorite—banana nut bread.

Breakfast
Scones

Combine first 5 ingredients in a medium bowl; stir well. Cut in butter with a pastry blender until mixture is crumbly. Add sour cream and egg, stirring just until dry ingredients are moistened. Stir in currants, if desired.

Turn dough out onto a lightly floured surface, and knead lightly 4 or 5 times. Pat dough into a 7-inch circle on a greased baking sheet. Brush top with milk; sprinkle with 1 tablespoon sugar. Cut circle into 6 wedges, using a sharp knife.

Bake at 400° for 14 to 16 minutes or until lightly browned. Serve scones warm with jam or honey butter. Yield: 6 scones.

◆

2 cups all-purpose flour

2 teaspoons baking powder

½ teaspoon baking soda

¼ teaspoon salt

3 tablespoons sugar

⅓ cup butter or margarine

½ cup sour cream

1 large egg, lightly beaten

⅔ cup currants (optional)

2 teaspoons milk

1 tablespoon sugar

◆

Italian
Cinnamon Sticks

¾ cup sugar

½ cup walnuts, ground

1 teaspoon ground cinnamon

1 cup butter or margarine, softened

1 (8-ounce) package cream cheese, softened

2½ cups all-purpose flour

1 large egg, lightly beaten

Combine first 3 ingredients in a small bowl; stir well, and set aside.

Beat butter and cream cheese at medium speed of an electric mixer until creamy. Gradually add flour, beating at low speed until blended. Shape dough into a ball; wrap in plastic wrap, and chill 30 minutes.

Divide dough in half; place 1 portion between 2 sheets of lightly floured wax paper, and roll into a 10-inch square (about ⅛ inch thick). Brush with egg; sprinkle with half of sugar mixture. Cut into 5- x ½-inch strips; twist strips, and place on ungreased baking sheets. Repeat procedure with remaining dough, egg, and sugar mixture.

Bake at 350° for 10 to 12 minutes or until golden. Remove to wire racks to cool. Yield: about 6½ dozen.

Pair these Italian-inspired pastries with a rich, bold coffee such as Barnie's Golden Espresso Blend™ or Ethiopian Yrgacheffe.

Beyond the Coffee Break

Chocolate

Hazelnut Biscotti

2⅔ cups all-purpose flour

1½ teaspoons baking soda

¼ teaspoon salt

2 cups sugar

1 cup cocoa

3 large eggs

3 egg whites

1 tablespoon finely ground espresso beans

1½ teaspoons Barnie's Hazelnut Flavoring Syrup

1½ cups whole hazelnuts, toasted and skinned

⅔ cup semisweet chocolate morsels

Combine first 5 ingredients in a large bowl; stir well. Combine eggs, egg whites, espresso, and flavoring syrup, stirring well with a wire whisk. Slowly add egg mixture to flour mixture, stirring until dry ingredients are moistened. Stir in hazelnuts and chocolate morsels (mixture will be very stiff).

Place dough on a lightly floured surface, and divide into 3 portions. Lightly flour hands, and shape each portion into a 7-inch log. Place logs 4 inches apart on lightly greased cookie sheets. Bake at 325° for 45 minutes. Cool logs completely on a wire rack. Reduce oven temperature to 300°.

Using a serrated knife, carefully cut each log crosswise into ½-inch slices. Place slices on ungreased cookie sheets. Bake at 300° for 20 minutes. Cool completely on wire racks. Yield: 3½ dozen.

Biscotti, the twice-baked Italian classic, is intensely crunchy—suitable for dunking into a cup of steaming Barnie's Espresso Roast.

(Photograph of Chocolate Hazelnut Biscotti and Perfect Almond Biscotti on preceding page)

Perfect
Almond Biscotti

Combine first 5 ingredients in a large bowl; stir well. Combine eggs, egg whites, flavoring syrup, and vanilla, stirring well with a wire whisk. Slowly add egg mixture to flour mixture, stirring until dry ingredients are moistened. Stir in almonds.

Place dough on a lightly floured surface, and divide into 3 portions. Lightly flour hands, and shape each portion into a 7-inch log. Place logs 4 inches apart on lightly greased cookie sheets. Bake at 350° for 35 to 40 minutes or until lightly browned. Let cool 15 minutes. Reduce oven temperature to 300°.

Using a serrated knife, carefully cut each log crosswise into ½-inch slices. Place slices on ungreased cookie sheets. Bake at 300° for 15 to 20 minutes. Cool completely on wire racks. Yield: 3½ dozen.

This almond-flavored biscotti is ideal for dipping into a frothy cup of cappuccino.

◆

4 cups all-purpose flour

1 teaspoon baking powder

½ teaspoon salt

1⅔ cups sugar

1½ tablespoons grated orange rind

3 large eggs

3 egg whites

2 teaspoons Barnie's Almond Flavoring Syrup

1 teaspoon vanilla extract

1½ cups whole natural almonds, toasted

◆

Lemon
Tea Bread

◆

1 (8-ounce) package cream cheese, softened

½ cup butter or margarine, softened

1¼ cups sugar

2 large eggs

2¼ cups all-purpose flour

1 tablespoon baking powder

½ teaspoon salt

¾ cup milk

⅔ cup finely chopped almonds, toasted

1 tablespoon grated lemon rind, divided

⅔ cup sifted powdered sugar

2 tablespoons lemon juice

Garnish: lemon zest

Beat cream cheese and butter at high speed of an electric mixer until light and fluffy. Gradually add 1¼ cups sugar, beating well. Add eggs, one at a time, beating well after each addition.

Combine flour, baking powder, and salt; add to creamed mixture alternately with milk, beginning and ending with flour mixture. Mix after each addition. Stir in almonds and 2 teaspoons lemon rind.

Pour batter evenly into two greased and floured 8½- x 4½- x 3-inch loafpans. Bake at 350° for 45 to 50 minutes or until a wooden pick inserted in center comes out clean.

Combine powdered sugar and lemon juice, stirring until smooth. Stir in remaining 1 teaspoon lemon rind. Spoon glaze over warm loaves. Let cool in pans 10 minutes. Remove from pans, and let cool completely on wire racks. Garnish, if desired. Yield: 2 loaves.

Accompany this slightly sweet quick loaf with Barnie's Lemon & Spice Tea to double the citrus appeal. Give the second loaf to a friend.

◆

Buttery
Chocolate Chip Scones

◆

4 cups sifted cake flour

2 tablespoons baking powder

1½ teaspoons salt

2 tablespoons sugar

½ cup unsalted butter

1 cup semisweet chocolate morsels

2 cups heavy whipping cream

◆

Combine first 4 ingredients in a large bowl. Cut in butter with a pastry blender until mixture is crumbly. Add chocolate morsels, stirring well. Add whipping cream, stirring until dry ingredients are moistened. Turn dough out onto a lightly floured surface, and knead 3 or 4 times.

Roll dough to ¾-inch thickness; cut with a 2-inch round cutter. Place scones on a lightly greased baking sheet. Bake at 400° for 15 minutes or until golden. Yield: about 2 dozen.

Afternoon tea is at its prime when you display these delectable scones; they're made extra fluffy with the addition of whipping cream. Pour a cup of Barnie's Cinnamon Butter Cookie Coffee as a tea alternative.

Anna, 7th Duchess of Bedford, is to be credited with the invention of afternoon tea, originally known as "Low Tea." Every afternoon between the morning meal and the late meal, often taken as late as nine o'clock, a sinking feeling overcame Anna. Therefore, one afternoon in 1840 she asked for a tray of bread and butter, cake and tea. Enjoying it so, she began to invite her friends who quickly caught on to the idea. As time passed, afternoon tea became an increasingly elaborate social event.

Rich

Brownie Cupcakes

Place butter and chocolates in a heavy saucepan; cook over low heat, stirring constantly, until melted. Remove from heat; stir in sugar. Add eggs, one at a time, stirring well after each addition; stir in vanilla.

Combine flour, cocoa, and salt; add to chocolate mixture, stirring with a wire whisk until smooth. Stir in pecans. Spoon batter into paper-lined muffin pans, filling three-fourths full. Bake at 350° for 35 minutes. Yield: 16 cupcakes.

Kids will welcome a glass of cold milk with these fudgy cupcakes, while adults may choose Barnie's Puerto Rican Yauco Selecto Coffee to draw out the intense chocolate flavor.

◆

¾ cup butter or margarine

2 (1-ounce) squares semisweet chocolate

1 (1-ounce) square unsweetened chocolate

1¾ cups sugar

4 large eggs

1 teaspoon vanilla extract

1 cup all-purpose flour

2 tablespoons Dutch process cocoa

⅛ teaspoon salt

1 cup chopped pecans, toasted

◆

Chocolate-Almond

Petits Fours

¾ cup butter, softened

2 (8-ounce) cans almond paste

1½ cups sugar

8 large eggs

1½ cups all-purpose flour

1 (12-ounce) can apricot filling

Chocolate Ganache

6 ounces white chocolate, melted

Garnish: white chocolate shavings

Grease bottom and sides of two 15- x 10- x 1-inch jellyroll pans, and line with wax paper; grease and flour wax paper. Set aside.

Beat butter and almond paste at medium speed of an electric mixer until creamy. Gradually add sugar; beat well. Add eggs, one at a time, beating after each addition. Stir in flour. Spread batter into prepared pans. Bake at 400° for 8 to 10 minutes. Cool in pans on wire racks. Turn one cake out onto a flat surface; remove wax paper, and spread with apricot filling. Top with remaining cake, bottom side up; cut with a 1¾-inch round (or other shaped) cutter.

Place small cakes on a wire rack in a large, shallow pan. Slowly spoon warm Chocolate Ganache over cakes, coating tops and sides evenly. (Spoon up excess ganache that drips through rack; reheat and use to continue frosting cakes.) Chill cakes 10 minutes. Pipe dots or designs on frosted cakes with melted white chocolate. Garnish, if desired. Yield: 3½ dozen.

Chocolate Ganache

1½ cups whipping cream

16 (1-ounce) squares semisweet chocolate, chopped

Bring whipping cream to a simmer in a heavy saucepan over medium heat. Remove from heat; add chocolate. Let stand 1 minute. Stir gently until chocolate melts and mixture is smooth. Yield: 3 cups.

Java
Gingerbread

1 (14.5-ounce) package
  gingerbread mix

1 cup brewed Barnie's
  Premium Blend Coffee,
  lukewarm

1 large egg, lightly beaten

½ cup chopped pecans

Orange Cream Frosting

Garnish: orange zest

2 (3-ounce) packages
  cream cheese, softened

½ teaspoon grated orange
  rind

2 tablespoons orange juice

1 cup sifted powdered
  sugar

Combine first 3 ingredients in an ungreased 8-inch square pan. Stir with a fork until batter is blended. Stir in pecans.

  Bake at 350° for 30 to 35 minutes or until a wooden pick inserted in center comes out clean. Let cool completely in pan. Spread Orange Cream Frosting over gingerbread. Garnish, if desired. Yield: 9 servings.

Orange Cream Frosting

Beat cream cheese at medium speed of an electric mixer until smooth. Add orange rind and juice. Gradually add sugar, beating until light and fluffy. Yield: ½ cup.

Gingerbread mix gives you a jump start for this easy yet impressive recipe. Barnie's Cinnamon & Spice Coffee is just the right accompaniment.

Marbled
Peanut Butter Fudge

Combine first 3 ingredients in a large heavy saucepan; bring to a boil, and cook, stirring constantly, 8 minutes. Add marshmallow cream, chocolate morsels, and vanilla; stir until blended.

Pour two-thirds of mixture into a buttered 13- x 9- x 2-inch pan; dollop with peanut butter. Spoon remaining chocolate mixture over peanut butter; gently swirl mixture with a knife to create a marbled effect. Chill until set. Cut into 1½-inch pieces. Store in an airtight container in refrigerator. Yield: 5 pounds.

A bold, full-bodied blend such as Barnie's Ethiopian Yrgacheffe Coffee accents the dynamic duo of peanut butter and chocolate in this creamy fudge.

◆

4 cups sugar

1 (12-ounce) can evaporated milk

1 cup butter or margarine

1 (7-ounce) jar marshmallow cream

3 (6-ounce) packages semisweet chocolate morsels

1 tablespoon vanilla extract

1 cup peanut butter

◆

Café au Lait

Pralines

1½ cups sugar

1½ cups coarsely chopped pecans

¾ cup firmly packed brown sugar

¼ cup plus 2 tablespoons butter

½ cup milk

1½ tablespoons finely ground espresso beans

Vegetable cooking spray

Combine first 6 ingredients in a heavy 3-quart saucepan. Bring to a boil over medium heat, stirring constantly. Boil, uncovered, stirring constantly, 1 to 2 minutes or until a candy thermometer registers 220°.

Immediately remove mixture from heat, and beat with a wooden spoon 4 to 6 minutes or just until mixture begins to thicken. Working rapidly, drop by tablespoonfuls onto wax paper coated with cooking spray; let stand until firm. Yield: 2½ dozen.

A hint of ground espresso sprinkles extra flavor into this classic candy. Pralines are at their finest when served with a Barnie's dark roast coffee.

Where coffee is served there is grace and splendor and friendship and happiness. All cares vanish as the coffee cup is raised to the lips.

—Abd-al-Kadir, *In Praise of Coffee*, 1587

Candy Bar
Cookies

Beat shortening at medium speed of an electric mixer 2 minutes or until creamy; gradually add brown sugar, beating at medium speed 5 minutes. Add egg, beating well.

Combine flour and next 5 ingredients. Add to shortening mixture, beating at low speed just until combined. Stir in chopped candy bars and vanilla. Chill dough 30 minutes.

Shape dough into 1½-inch balls; place 2 inches apart on ungreased cookie sheets. Bake at 350° for 8 to 10 minutes (cookies will be soft). Cool slightly on cookie sheets; remove to wire racks to cool completely. Yield: about 3 dozen.

Chock-full of chopped candy bars, these irresistible cookies will lure anyone's hand back into the cookie jar.

⅔ cup butter-flavored shortening

1¼ cups firmly packed brown sugar

1 large egg

1½ cups all-purpose flour

1 teaspoon baking powder

½ teaspoon baking soda

¼ teaspoon salt

½ cup regular oats, uncooked

½ teaspoon ground cinnamon

4 (2.07-ounce) chocolate coated caramel-peanut nougat bars, coarsely chopped

1 teaspoon vanilla extract

Orange
Cookies

◆

1 cup shortening

1 cup sugar

1 large egg

1 tablespoon grated orange rind

1 tablespoon orange juice

2¼ cups all-purpose flour

1 teaspoon baking powder

Pinch of salt

1 cup chopped pecans

◆

Beat shortening at medium speed of an electric mixer until fluffy; gradually add sugar, beating well. Add egg, orange rind, and orange juice; beat well.

Combine flour, baking powder, and salt. Add to egg mixture, beating just until blended. Stir in pecans. Shape dough into a 15-inch-long roll; wrap in wax paper, and chill 2 hours or until dough is firm.

Unwrap roll, and cut into ¼-inch slices; place on lightly greased cookie sheets. Bake at 375° for 15 to 17 minutes or until lightly browned. Cool on wire racks. Yield: 3 dozen.

These orange-scented cookies resemble shortbread in texture. The dough can be made ahead and chilled. Then just slice and bake—and serve with Barnie's Orange & Spice Tea.

Tea first became available to the public in London at Garway's Coffee House in 1657. Customers were assured that a sip of the brew "vanquisheth heavy dreams, easeth the Brain, and strengtheneth the Memory." Its popularity grew and soon other London coffeehouses made tea available to their patrons.

Toasted Almond
and Cranberry Cookies

Beat butter and shortening at medium speed of an electric mixer until soft and creamy. Gradually add sugars, beating well. Add eggs, mixing well.

Combine flour, baking powder, soda, and salt. Add to butter mixture, beating just until blended. Stir in white chocolate and remaining ingredients.

Drop dough by tablespoonfuls 2 inches apart onto ungreased cookie sheets. Bake at 350° for 10 minutes. Cool on wire racks. Yield: 6 dozen.

Dried cranberries and creamy white chocolate give these cookies their jeweled appearance. Barnie's Amaretto Tea or French Vanilla Coffee provides the crowning touch for an afternoon snack.

◆

½ cup butter or margarine, softened

½ cup shortening

1 cup firmly packed brown sugar

⅔ cup sugar

2 large eggs

2 cups all-purpose flour

1 teaspoon baking powder

½ teaspoon baking soda

⅛ teaspoon salt

8 ounces premium white chocolate, chopped

2 cups corn flakes cereal

1 cup sliced almonds, toasted

2 (3-ounce) packages dried cranberries

¾ teaspoon almond extract

White Chocolate

Macadamia Nut Cookies

½ cup butter or margarine, softened

½ cup shortening

¾ cup firmly packed brown sugar

½ cup sugar

1 large egg

1½ teaspoons vanilla extract

2 cups all-purpose flour

1 teaspoon baking soda

½ teaspoon salt

1 (7-ounce) jar macadamia nuts, coarsely chopped

1 (6-ounce) package white chocolate-flavored baking bars, cut into chunks

Beat butter and shortening at medium speed of an electric mixer until soft and creamy; gradually add sugars, beating well. Add egg and vanilla; beat well.

Combine flour, soda, and salt; gradually add to butter mixture, beating well. Stir in macadamia nuts and white chocolate.

Drop dough by rounded teaspoonfuls 2 inches apart onto lightly greased cookie sheets. Bake at 350° for 8 to 10 minutes or until lightly browned. Cool slightly on cookie sheets; remove to wire racks, and let cool completely. Yield: 5 dozen.

Laden with buttery macadamia nuts and white chocolate, these million-dollar cookies meet their match with a cup of Barnie's White Chocolate Mousse or Chocolate Macadamia Nut Coffee.

Blonde

Shortbread

Beat butter and espresso at medium speed of an electric mixer until creamy; gradually add powdered sugar, beating well. Stir in flour.

Press dough evenly into two ungreased 9-inch round cakepans. Bake at 350° for 10 minutes or until lightly browned. Let cool slightly in pans. Cut shortbread into wedges. Carefully remove shortbread from pans.

Dip wide ends of cookies into candy coating, and then into chopped pecans. Place on wax paper until set. Yield: 2 dozen.

Blonde Shortbread and Coconut Shortbread Hearts (page 52) make any afternoon special.

◆

1 cup butter, softened

2 teaspoons finely ground espresso beans

2/3 cup sifted powdered sugar

2 cups all-purpose flour

3 ounces vanilla-flavored candy coating, melted

1/2 cup chopped pecans, toasted

◆

Coconut

Shortbread Hearts

◆

¾ cup butter, softened

⅓ cup sugar

1½ teaspoons vanilla extract

1¾ cups all-purpose flour

½ teaspoon baking powder

¼ teaspoon salt

1 cup flaked coconut

1 (6-ounce) package
semisweet chocolate
morsels

2 teaspoons shortening

Flaked coconut, toasted

◆

Beat butter at medium speed of an electric mixer until creamy; gradually add sugar, beating well. Stir in vanilla. Combine flour, baking powder, and salt; gradually add to butter mixture, mixing well. Stir in 1 cup coconut. Cover and chill 1 hour.

Roll dough to ¼-inch thickness on a lightly floured surface. Cut dough into heart shapes with a 3-inch cookie cutter, and place on lightly greased cookie sheets. Bake at 300° for 25 to 30 minutes or until edges are lightly browned. Remove cookies to wire racks to cool.

Melt chocolate morsels and shortening in a small heavy saucepan over medium-low heat. Dip edges of cookies in chocolate mixture; then dip in toasted coconut. Place on cookie sheets lined with wax paper. Chill 10 minutes. Yield: 2 dozen.

Offer these buttery rich, coconut-laced cookies (photographed on preceding page) with Café Viennese featured on page 91.

Mud Slide

Mocha Malts

Combine milk and espresso, stirring until espresso dissolves. Pour half of milk mixture into container of an electric blender; add half each of ice cream, fudge topping, malted milk, and liqueur. Cover and process until smooth, stopping once to scrape down sides. Stir in half of chopped cookies. Spoon malts into glasses.

Place remaining half of milk mixture, ice cream, fudge topping, malted milk, and liqueur in container of electric blender. Cover and process until smooth. Stir in remaining chopped cookies. Spoon into glasses. Serve immediately. Yield: 6 (1-cup) servings.

This malt meets every requirement for a sinfully rich beverage or dessert.

1 cup milk

1 teaspoon finely ground espresso beans

6 cups vanilla ice cream, divided

½ cup commercial hot fudge topping, divided

½ cup chocolate-flavored instant malted milk, divided

¼ cup Kahlúa or Barnie's Decadent Dark Chocolate Coffee Cooler®

6 cream-filled chocolate sandwich cookies, coarsely chopped and divided

Sage-Pecan
Cheese Wafers

1 cup (4 ounces) shredded sharp Cheddar cheese

¾ cup all-purpose flour

¼ cup chopped pecans

1 teaspoon rubbed sage

¼ teaspoon salt

⅛ teaspoon ground red pepper

⅓ cup butter or margarine, cut into small pieces

Pecan halves (optional)

Position knife blade in food processor bowl; add first 6 ingredients. Process 10 seconds or until blended. Slowly drop butter, one piece at a time, through food chute with processor running, blending just until mixture forms a ball.

Roll dough to ¼-inch thickness on a lightly floured surface. Cut with a 1½-inch round cutter, and place on ungreased baking sheets. Top with pecan halves, if desired. Bake at 350° for 12 to 14 minutes or until edges are golden. Remove to wire racks to cool. Yield: 3 dozen.

A cup of espresso, the purist's coffee, brings out the spicy blend of seasonings and pecans in this variation of a cheese straw.

Sweet and Spicy

Pecans

Toss pecans in butter. Combine sugar and remaining ingredients. Sprinkle over pecans; toss to coat. Spread coated pecans on a greased baking sheet.

Bake at 325° for 15 minutes, stirring every 5 minutes. Let cool completely. Store in an airtight container. Yield: 2 cups.

A cup of Barnie's Peaches 'n' Cream® Tea or full-bodied Mocha Java Coffee and these spiced nuts make a sensational combination.

The most famous story of the birth of coffee is the legend of Khaldi, a goatherder, who in 850 A.D. saw his flock prancing around the plains of Ethiopia. He noticed that the goats were eating a strange berry, and resolved to try one himself. He found that he, too, was suddenly happy, excited, and clear thinking. A passing monk was astonished to see the usually melancholy herdsman merrily dancing with his flock. After learning Khaldi's secret, the monk dried the fruit in the fire and boiled it in water and used this new drink to stay awake for nightlong religious services.

◆

2 cups pecan halves

2 tablespoons butter or margarine, melted

1 tablespoon sugar

1 teaspoon ground cumin

1 teaspoon chili powder

½ teaspoon dried crushed red pepper

¼ teaspoon salt

◆

Curried
Chicken Salad Cream Puffs

◆

2 (3-ounce) packages
    cream cheese, softened

½ cup plain yogurt

1 tablespoon plus 1
    teaspoon curry powder

1 tablespoon lemon juice

¼ teaspoon salt

⅛ teaspoon ground red
    pepper

1½ cups finely chopped
    cooked chicken

½ cup raisins

½ cup finely chopped
    almonds, toasted

⅓ cup flaked coconut

    Miniature Cream Puffs
    (facing page)

◆

Beat cream cheese in a large bowl at medium speed of an electric mixer until smooth. Add yogurt, curry powder, lemon juice, salt, and pepper; mix well. Stir in chicken, raisins, almonds, and coconut. Cover and chill thoroughly.

Just before serving, cut off top one-third of each Miniature Cream Puff; pull out and discard soft dough inside. Spoon 1 level tablespoon chicken mixture into each cream puff; replace tops. Yield: 2½ dozen.

This Indian-spiced chicken salad can also star as a main-dish luncheon salad. Serve it in a pineapple shell or on curly leaf lettuce.

Miniature Cream Puffs

Combine water and butter in a medium saucepan; bring to a boil. Combine flour and salt. Add to butter mixture, all at once, stirring vigorously over medium-high heat until mixture leaves sides of pan and forms a smooth ball. Remove from heat, and let cool 4 to 5 minutes.

Add eggs, one at a time, beating thoroughly with a wooden spoon after each addition; then beat until dough is smooth.

Spoon mixture into a decorating bag fitted with a No. 5 or 6B large fluted tip. Pipe mixture into 30 small balls on lightly greased baking sheets. Bake at 400° for 20 minutes or until puffed and golden. Cool on a wire rack away from drafts. Yield: 2½ dozen miniature cream puffs.

⅔ cup water

⅓ cup butter or margarine

⅔ cup all-purpose flour

⅛ teaspoon salt

3 large eggs

As the popularity of coffee drinking grew during the seventeenth century, the coffeehouse became the hub of political and cultural life in London, even though the House of Commons declared coffee an "outlandish drink."

Cucumber
Party Sandwiches

1 medium onion

1 large cucumber, peeled, seeded, and quartered

2 (8-ounce) packages cream cheese, softened

½ teaspoon salt

⅛ teaspoon ground white pepper

40 (¼-inch-thick) slices white bread

40 (¼-inch-thick) slices whole wheat bread

1 (8-ounce) package cream cheese, softened

1 tablespoon milk

1 tablespoon minced fresh dillweed

Garnishes: radish slices, fresh dillweed sprigs

Quarter onion. Position knife blade in food processor bowl; add onion and cucumber. Process 10 seconds or until finely chopped, scraping sides of bowl once. Drain well on paper towels.

Return blade to processor bowl. Place 2 packages cream cheese in bowl. Process 10 seconds or until smooth. Drop cucumber mixture, salt, and pepper through food chute with processor running; process 25 seconds or until blended, scraping sides of bowl once. Cover and chill.

Cut white bread slices into 40 rounds with a 2½-inch cutter. Repeat procedure with wheat bread. Spread 1 tablespoon cream cheese mixture on one side of each white bread round; top each with a wheat bread round. Turn half of the sandwiches wheat bread side up.

Combine 1 package cream cheese, milk, and minced dillweed in a small bowl; stir until blended. Spoon cream cheese mixture into a decorating bag fitted with a No. 4 tip. Pipe a rosette of cream cheese mixture onto each sandwich. Garnish, if desired. Yield: 40 appetizers.

Showcase these fancy finger sandwiches on a tiered pedestal for an afternoon tea party along with Barnie's Gold-Tipped Darjeeling Tea.

Scrumptious Endings

Mississippi Mud

Brownies

4 (1-ounce) squares
   unsweetened chocolate

1 cup butter or margarine

2 cups sugar

1 cup all-purpose flour

⅛ teaspoon salt

4 large eggs, beaten

1 cup chopped pecans

2 (1-ounce) squares
   unsweetened chocolate

½ cup evaporated milk

½ cup butter or margarine

½ teaspoon vanilla extract

4½ to 5 cups sifted powdered
   sugar

3 cups miniature
   marshmallows

Combine 4 squares chocolate and 1 cup butter in a large saucepan; cook over low heat, stirring until chocolate and butter melt. Remove mixture from heat.

Combine 2 cups sugar, flour, and salt; add to chocolate mixture. Add eggs and pecans; stir until blended. Spoon batter into a lightly greased and floured 13- x 9- x 2-inch pan.

Bake at 350° for 25 to 30 minutes or just until a wooden pick inserted in center comes out clean.

Meanwhile, combine 2 squares chocolate, milk, and ½ cup butter in a heavy saucepan. Cook over low heat, stirring often, until chocolate and butter melt. Remove from heat. Transfer to a medium bowl. Stir in vanilla. Gradually add powdered sugar, beating at low speed of an electric mixer until frosting is smooth.

Sprinkle marshmallows evenly over warm brownies. Quickly pour frosting over marshmallows, spreading evenly. Let cool completely, and cut into bars. Yield: 2 dozen.

(Photograph of Mississippi Mud Brownies on preceding page)

Raspberry

Brownies

Beat butter at medium speed of an electric mixer until soft and creamy; gradually add sugar, beating well. Add eggs and chocolate, mixing well. Add flour to butter mixture, mixing well; stir in walnuts.

Spoon half of batter into a greased and floured 9-inch square pan. Spread raspberry jam over batter; top with remaining batter. Bake at 350° for 28 to 30 minutes. Cool on a wire rack. Cut into squares. Yield: 3 dozen.

A warming cup of Barnie's Vanilla Cream Coffee flatters these jam-filled chocolate squares.

½ cup butter or margarine, softened

1 cup sugar

2 large eggs

2 (1-ounce) squares unsweetened chocolate, melted

¾ cup all-purpose flour

1 cup chopped walnuts

⅓ cup raspberry jam

It's "lovelier than a thousand kisses, sweeter than muscatel wine. There's no way to please me except with coffee."
— J.S. Bach, *Coffee Cantata*

Kahlúa

Truffle Sticks

2 tablespoons sugar

1 (4-ounce) bar Swiss dark
  chocolate, chopped

3 (1-ounce) squares
  unsweetened chocolate,
  chopped

¼ cup plus 2 tablespoons
  butter or margarine,
  softened and divided

¾ cup sugar

2 large eggs

⅔ cup all-purpose flour

¼ teaspoon salt

⅓ cup Kahlúa

½ cup semisweet chocolate
  mini-morsels

Line a greased 8-inch square pan with foil, allowing foil to extend over edges. Butter foil; sprinkle 2 tablespoons sugar onto foil.

Combine chopped chocolates and 2 tablespoons butter in top of a double boiler; bring water to a boil. Reduce heat to low; cook until chocolate and butter melt. Remove from heat, and let cool.

Beat remaining ¼ cup butter at medium speed of an electric mixer 2 minutes. Gradually add ¾ cup sugar, beating at medium speed 5 minutes. Add eggs, one at a time, beating after each addition until blended.

Combine flour and salt; add to butter mixture alternately with melted chocolate mixture and Kahlúa, beginning and ending with flour mixture. Mix at low speed just until blended. Stir in mini-morsels.

Spoon batter into prepared pan. Bake at 350° for 18 minutes (do not overbake). Cool completely. Cover and chill at least 2 hours.

To serve, lift foil out of pan, and cut brownies into 2- x 1-inch sticks. Yield: 32 brownies.

This deep, dark indulgence is a chocolate-lover's dream. Cap it off with an espresso or a Velvet Hammer (page 92).

Peanut Butter
Cheesecake

Combine cookie crumbs and butter; firmly press onto bottom and 1 inch up sides of a lightly greased 10-inch springform pan. Bake at 350° for 8 minutes. Let cool on a wire rack.

Beat cream cheese at medium speed of an electric mixer until fluffy; gradually add brown sugar, beating well. Add ¾ cup peanut butter, beating well. Add eggs, one at a time, beating after each addition. Stir in chopped candy and vanilla. (Mixture will be very thick.) Pour into prepared pan.

Bake at 350° for 40 to 45 minutes or until barely set.

Combine sour cream, ¼ cup peanut butter, and ¼ cup sugar, stirring until sugar dissolves. Spread sour cream mixture over warm cheesecake. Bake at 500° for 5 minutes. Cool completely on a wire rack. Cover and chill 8 hours. Remove sides of pan before serving. Yield: one 10-inch cheesecake.

The combination of a creamy, candy-flecked filling and a peanut butter cookie crust gives this cheesecake heavenly ratings.

2 cups cream-filled peanut butter sandwich cookie crumbs

¼ cup butter or margarine, melted

5 (8-ounce) packages cream cheese, softened

1½ cups firmly packed brown sugar

¾ cup creamy peanut butter

3 large eggs

1 cup chopped peanut butter cup candies

2 teaspoons vanilla extract

1 (16-ounce) carton sour cream

¼ cup creamy peanut butter

¼ cup sugar

Caramel-Brownie
Cheesecake

Combine vanilla wafer crumbs and butter; firmly press onto bottom and 2 inches up sides of a lightly greased 9-inch springform pan. Bake at 350° for 5 minutes. Let cool on a wire rack.

Combine caramels and milk in a small heavy saucepan; cook over low heat, stirring often, until caramels melt. Pour caramel mixture over crust. Sprinkle crumbled brownies over caramel.

Beat cream cheese at medium speed of an electric mixer 2 minutes or until fluffy. Gradually add brown sugar, mixing well. Add eggs, one at a time, beating after each addition just until blended. Stir in sour cream and vanilla.

Pour batter over brownies in crust. Bake at 350° for 50 minutes to 1 hour or until almost set. Remove from oven; let cool to room temperature on a wire rack. Cover and chill at least 4 hours. Remove sides of pan. Garnish, if desired. Yield: one 9-inch cheesecake.

Note: Buy prepackaged unfrosted brownies from a bakery, or prepare your favorite mix; let cool, and crumble enough to yield 2½ cups.

Caramel Nut Mocha (page 92) and a drizzle of commercial caramel topping on each plate echo the flavor blend in this extravagant caramel cheesecake.

◆

1¾ cups vanilla wafer crumbs

⅓ cup butter or margarine, melted

1 (14-ounce) package caramels

1 (5-ounce) can evaporated milk

2½ cups coarsely crumbled unfrosted brownies

3 (8-ounce) packages cream cheese, softened

1 cup firmly packed brown sugar

3 large eggs

1 (8-ounce) carton sour cream

2 teaspoons vanilla extract

Garnishes: whipped cream, chocolate-lined wafer rolls, chocolate coffee beans

Hot Fudge
Cheesecake

1 cup crushed saltine crackers

½ cup finely chopped walnuts

¼ cup plus 2 tablespoons butter or margarine, melted

3 tablespoons sugar

6 (1-ounce) squares semisweet chocolate

¾ cup butter or margarine

1 (8-ounce) package cream cheese, softened

¾ cup sugar

3 large eggs

Hot Fudge Sauce (facing page)

Garnishes: sweetened whipped cream, fresh mint sprigs

Combine first 4 ingredients; firmly press onto bottom and 2½ inches up sides of a lightly greased 7-inch springform pan. Bake at 350° for 10 minutes. Let cool on a wire rack. Reduce oven temperature to 300°.

Combine chocolate squares and ¾ cup butter in a heavy saucepan. Cook over medium-low heat until mixture is melted and smooth, stirring frequently. Remove from heat, and let cool.

Beat cream cheese at medium speed of an electric mixer until creamy. Add ¾ cup sugar; beat well. Add eggs, one at a time, beating after each addition. Stir in cooled chocolate mixture. Pour into prepared crust.

Bake at 300° for 50 minutes to 1 hour or until almost set. Turn oven off, and partially open door. Let cheesecake cool in oven 30 minutes. Remove to a wire rack; let cool to room temperature.

Remove sides of pan. Serve cheesecake with Hot Fudge Sauce. Garnish, if desired. Yield: one 7-inch cheesecake.

Hot Fudge Sauce

Combine chocolate morsels and half-and-half in a heavy saucepan. Cook over medium heat until chocolate melts and mixture is smooth, stirring frequently. Remove from heat; stir in butter and vanilla. Serve warm. Yield: 2 cups.

This cheesecake develops a brownie-like top as it bakes. The versatile Hot Fudge Sauce can also be served over pound cake, ice cream, or other cheesecakes.

◆

1 (12-ounce) package semisweet chocolate morsels

1 cup half-and-half

1 tablespoon butter or margarine

1 teaspoon vanilla extract

◆

In the early morning, while it was still dark and I was lying in bed, I heard the waggons loaded high up with coffee-sacks, 12 to a ton, with 16 oxen in each waggon starting on their way to Nairobi railway station up the long factory hill, with much shouting and rattling, the drivers running beside the waggons. The coffee would be on the sea in a day or two, and we could only hope for good luck at the big auction-sales in London.
—Baroness Karen Blixen, *Out of Africa*, 1937

Chocolate Dessert

in Crème Anglaise

16 (1-ounce) squares
   semisweet chocolate,
   chopped

⅔ cup butter or margarine

5 large eggs

2 tablespoons sugar

2 tablespoons all-purpose
   flour

Crème Anglaise

Garnishes: chocolate
   curls, fresh mint sprigs

◆

2 cups milk

½ cup sugar, divided

5 egg yolks

½ teaspoon vanilla extract

◆

Line the bottom of a 9-inch springform pan with parchment paper; set aside. Melt chopped chocolate and butter in a large heavy saucepan over medium-low heat, stirring often. Remove from heat, and let cool slightly. Gradually add chocolate mixture to eggs, beating at medium speed of an electric mixer 10 minutes. Fold in sugar and flour. Pour mixture into prepared pan.

Bake at 400° for 15 minutes. (Cake will not be set in center.) Remove from oven. Let cool; cover and chill thoroughly.

Spoon Crème Anglaise onto each individual dessert plate; place a wedge of chocolate on each plate. Garnish, if desired. Yield: 10 servings.

Crème Anglaise

Combine milk and ¼ cup sugar in a heavy nonaluminum saucepan. Bring to a simmer over medium heat. Beat remaining ¼ cup sugar and egg yolks at high speed of an electric mixer until pale and mixture forms a ribbon.

Gradually add hot milk mixture to egg mixture, whisking until blended; return to saucepan. Cook over medium-low heat, stirring constantly, until custard thickens and coats a spoon. Remove from heat; strain. Stir in vanilla. Cover and chill. Yield: 2 cups.

Milk Chocolate
Pound Cake

1 cup butter or margarine, softened

1½ cups sugar

4 large eggs

6 (1.55-ounce) milk chocolate candy bars, melted

2½ cups all-purpose flour

¼ teaspoon baking soda

Pinch of salt

1 cup buttermilk

1 cup chopped pecans

1 (5½-ounce) can chocolate syrup

2 teaspoons vanilla extract

Powdered sugar (optional)

Beat butter at medium speed of an electric mixer about 2 minutes or until soft and creamy. Gradually add 1½ cups sugar, beating at medium speed 5 to 7 minutes. Add eggs, one at a time, beating just until yellow disappears. Stir in melted candy bars.

Combine flour, soda, and salt in a small bowl; add to chocolate mixture alternately with buttermilk, beginning and ending with flour mixture. Mix at low speed after each addition just until blended. Add pecans, chocolate syrup, and vanilla, blending well.

Pour batter into a greased and floured 10-inch Bundt or tube pan. Bake at 325° for 1 hour and 15 minutes or until a wooden pick inserted in center comes out clean. Cool in pan 10 to 15 minutes; remove from pan, and let cool completely on a wire rack. Sift a small amount of powdered sugar over cake, if desired. Yield: one 10-inch cake.

Pound cake is one of America's favorite comfort foods. Try this milk chocolate version with Barnie's Cookies 'n' Cream Coffee.

Old-Fashioned
Buttermilk Pound Cake

Beat butter and shortening at medium speed of an electric mixer about 2 minutes or until soft and creamy. Gradually add sugar, beating at medium speed 5 to 7 minutes. Add eggs, one at a time, beating just until yellow disappears.

Dissolve soda in buttermilk. Combine flour and salt; add to creamed mixture alternately with buttermilk mixture, beginning and ending with flour mixture. Mix at low speed after each addition just until blended. Stir in flavorings.

Pour batter into a greased and floured 10-inch tube pan. Bake at 350° for 1 hour or until a wooden pick inserted in center comes out clean. Cool in pan 10 to 15 minutes; remove from pan, and let cool completely on a wire rack. Yield: one 10-inch cake.

½ cup butter or margarine, softened

½ cup shortening

2 cups sugar

4 large eggs

½ teaspoon baking soda

1 cup buttermilk

3 cups all-purpose flour

⅛ teaspoon salt

2 teaspoons lemon extract

1 teaspoon almond extract

◆

Pair Barnie's Honey Tea with this traditional pound cake. The cake can also be baked in two 9- x 5- x 3-inch loafpans. Bake at 350° for 45 to 50 minutes.

Banana-Pecan

Shortcake

1 cup butter or margarine, softened

¾ cup firmly packed brown sugar

1 teaspoon vanilla extract

2 cups all-purpose flour

1 cup ground pecans

⅛ teaspoon ground cinnamon

3 bananas, peeled and thinly sliced

2 tablespoons lemon juice

½ cup whipping cream

2 tablespoons brown sugar

1 cup sour cream

¼ cup coarsely chopped pecans, toasted

Beat butter at medium speed of an electric mixer until creamy; gradually add ¾ cup brown sugar, beating well. Stir in vanilla. Combine flour, ground pecans, and cinnamon; add to butter mixture, mixing until blended.

Divide dough in half. Place each portion of dough on a lightly greased baking sheet; roll each to ¼-inch thickness, and trim into 10-inch circles. Bake at 350° for 15 to 20 minutes. Cool 10 minutes on baking sheets; gently remove to wire racks, and cool completely.

Combine banana slices and lemon juice; set aside. Beat whipping cream and 2 tablespoons brown sugar until stiff peaks form; fold in sour cream. To serve, place a shortcake round on a serving plate; spread with half of whipped cream mixture, and arrange banana slices on top. Place remaining shortcake round over banana slices, and spread with remaining whipped cream mixture. Sprinkle with chopped pecans. Yield: one 2-layer shortcake.

Shortcake is a classic summertime dessert, particularly in the South. Enjoy this banana-filled version with one of Barnie's spiced teas.

Banana Split
Pudding Parfaits

Reserve 4 banana slices and 8 strawberry slices for garnish. Mash remaining banana until smooth. Beat mashed banana and 1 cup whipping cream in a mixing bowl at medium speed of an electric mixer until soft peaks form (mixture will not beat to stiff peaks). Gently fold in strawberry slices.

Combine fudge topping and peanut butter; stir well. Spoon banana pudding mixture evenly into four 8-ounce parfait glasses. Spoon fudge mixture over pudding. Top with reserved fruit slices, whipped cream, and cherries. Serve immediately. Yield: 4 servings.

You'll go bananas when you sample these fruit-filled pudding parfaits. Whip up a Banana Banshee Cappuccino (page 85) as an ideal accompaniment.

◆

3 large ripe bananas, sliced

1 cup fresh strawberries, hulled and sliced

1 cup whipping cream

¼ cup commercial hot fudge topping

2 tablespoons peanut butter

Sweetened whipped cream

Maraschino cherries

◆

Peppermint Fudge
Parfaits

Melt chocolate in top of a double boiler over hot, not simmering, water. Remove from heat; set aside.

Bring 1 cup whipping cream to a simmer in a small heavy saucepan. Combine eggs and egg yolks in a bowl. Beat lightly. Gradually add about one-fourth of hot cream to eggs, stirring constantly. Add to remaining hot cream. Cook over medium-low heat, stirring constantly, until mixture reaches 160°. Remove from heat; strain. Let cool.

Combine egg mixture, sugar, and peppermint extract in container of an electric blender; cover and process at medium-high speed 2 minutes. Add Kahlúa, and process 30 seconds. Add melted chocolate, and process until smooth.

Beat ¾ cup whipping cream until soft peaks form; fold in crushed peppermint candy.

Spoon 1 tablespoon cookie crumbs into each of four 8-ounce parfait glasses; top each with 2½ tablespoons chocolate mousse mixture and 2 tablespoons whipped cream mixture. Repeat layers, ending with whipped cream mixture. Cover and chill 8 hours. Garnish, if desired. Yield: 4 servings.

◆

6 (1-ounce) squares semisweet chocolate

1 cup whipping cream

2 large eggs

2 egg yolks

¼ cup sugar

½ teaspoon peppermint extract

3 tablespoons Kahlúa or Barnie's Decadent Dark Chocolate Coffee Cooler®

¾ cup whipping cream

¼ cup crushed peppermint candy

½ cup cream-filled chocolate sandwich cookie crumbs

Garnish: candy canes

◆

Coffee-Fudge
Sauce

1 (14-ounce) bag caramels

½ cup semisweet chocolate morsels

¼ cup brewed Barnie's Premium Blend Coffee or Latte Coffee Cooler®

¼ cup half-and-half

Combine all ingredients in a saucepan; cook over medium heat, stirring occasionally, until caramels and chocolate morsels melt. Serve warm or at room temperature over ice cream or pound cake. Yield: about 2 cups.

White Chocolate
Orange Sauce

1 (6-ounce) white chocolate-flavored baking bar

½ cup light corn syrup

¼ teaspoon grated orange rind

3 tablespoons orange juice or Barnie's Orange Flavoring Syrup

Combine first 3 ingredients in top of a double boiler; bring water to a boil. Reduce heat to low; cook until white chocolate melts, stirring frequently. Gradually add orange juice, stirring until smooth. Remove from heat. Serve at room temperature. Yield: 1¼ cups.

As an option, forego frosting Java Gingerbread (page 44) and try serving it with thick White Chocolate Orange Sauce (in foreground at right). Warm Coffee-Fudge Sauce (in background) pours nicely over vanilla ice cream.

Rum-Laced

Pecan Pie

1 cup sugar

1 cup light corn syrup

⅓ cup butter or margarine

4 large eggs, lightly beaten

3 tablespoons dark rum

1 teaspoon vanilla extract

¼ teaspoon salt

1 (15-ounce) package refrigerated piecrusts

1¼ cups pecan halves

Combine first 3 ingredients in a medium saucepan; cook over low heat, stirring constantly, until sugar dissolves and butter melts. Remove from heat; let cool slightly. Stir in eggs, rum, vanilla, and salt.

Place one piecrust in a 9-inch pieplate. Cut leaf shapes or other desired shapes from remaining piecrust, using cookie cutters. Arrange leaves around edge of pieplate, pressing gently.

Pour filling into prepared piecrust, and top with pecan halves. Bake at 325° for 1 hour and 10 minutes or until pie is set. Let cool completely. Yield: one 9-inch pie.

Experience the exotic flavor boost that dark rum lends to this rich pecan pie. Café Caribbean (page 90) will further enliven your tropical taste buds.

Ice Cream

Pie Spectacular

1 cup graham cracker
  crumbs

½ cup chopped walnuts

¼ cup plus 1 tablespoon
  butter or margarine,
  melted

1 pint coffee ice cream,
  softened

1 pint vanilla ice cream,
  softened

  Brown Sugar Sauce

◆

3 tablespoons butter or
  margarine

1 cup firmly packed brown
  sugar

½ cup half-and-half

1 cup chopped walnuts

1 teaspoon vanilla extract

◆

Combine first 3 ingredients, stirring well. Press mixture firmly into a buttered 9-inch pieplate. Bake at 375° for 8 minutes; let cool completely.

Spoon coffee ice cream into crust, spreading evenly; freeze until almost firm. Spread vanilla ice cream over coffee ice cream layer, and freeze until firm. Serve with warm Brown Sugar Sauce. Yield: one 9-inch pie.

Note: This frozen pie is a great make-ahead dessert. Just reheat Brown Sugar Sauce before serving.

Brown Sugar Sauce

Melt butter in a heavy saucepan over low heat; add brown sugar. Cook, stirring constantly, 5 to 6 minutes. Remove from heat, and gradually stir in half-and-half. Return pan to heat, and cook 1 minute. Remove from heat; stir in walnuts and vanilla. Yield: about 1½ cups.

Honey Cream
Cashew Tart

Roll piecrust into a 12-inch circle. Place in an ungreased 11-inch tart pan with removable bottom. Trim off excess dough around edges. Spread ¾ cup melted chocolate morsels over piecrust, and chill.

Combine brown sugar, butter, and honey in a medium saucepan; stir well. Cook over medium heat until butter melts and sugar dissolves. Bring to a boil; reduce heat, and simmer 2 minutes, stirring occasionally. Remove from heat; stir in 3 tablespoons whipping cream and vanilla. Let cool 15 minutes.

Add eggs, one at a time, beating with a wire whisk after each addition. Stir in cashews. Pour cashew mixture into piecrust. Bake at 350° for 20 minutes or until set. Let cool completely on a wire rack.

Combine white chocolate baking bar and 2 tablespoons whipping cream in top of a double boiler; bring water to a boil. Reduce heat to low; cook until white chocolate melts, stirring frequently. Pour white chocolate mixture over cooled tart.

Spoon ⅓ cup melted chocolate morsels in small circles over white chocolate mixture in center and around edge of tart. Pull tip of a wooden pick or knife through each circle, forming small hearts. Chill at least 10 minutes. To serve, carefully remove sides of tart pan. Yield: one 11-inch tart.

◆

½ (15-ounce) package refrigerated piecrusts

¾ cup semisweet chocolate morsels, melted

1 cup firmly packed brown sugar

½ cup butter or margarine

¼ cup honey

3 tablespoons whipping cream

1 tablespoon vanilla extract

2 large eggs

2 cups chopped cashews

1 (6-ounce) white chocolate-flavored baking bar

2 tablespoons whipping cream

⅓ cup semisweet chocolate morsels, melted

◆

Lemon

Macaroon Tarts

◆

2¼ cups sugar

¼ cup plus 1 tablespoon cornstarch

1½ teaspoons grated lemon rind

1 cup water

1 cup fresh lemon juice

3 large eggs, lightly beaten

Macaroon Tart Shells

Frozen whipped topping, thawed

Lemon zest

◆

4 cups flaked coconut

1 cup sugar

¾ cup all-purpose flour

2 teaspoons vanilla extract

3 egg whites

Combine first 3 ingredients in a heavy saucepan. Gradually add water and lemon juice; stir until blended. Cook over medium heat, stirring constantly, until thickened. Boil 1 minute, stirring constantly. Remove from heat.

Gradually stir about one-fourth of hot mixture into eggs; add to remaining hot mixture, stirring constantly. Cook over medium heat, stirring constantly, 1 minute or until thickened. Remove from heat. Let cool. Cover and chill thoroughly.

Spoon filling evenly into Macaroon Tart Shells. Top each with whipped topping and lemon zest. Store in an airtight container in refrigerator up to 1 week. Yield: 20 tarts.

Macaroon Tart Shells

Combine all ingredients; stir well. Spoon mixture evenly into 20 greased muffin cups, pressing into bottom and up sides of cups. Bake at 400° for 13 to 15 minutes or until edges are browned. Cool in pans on wire racks 2 minutes. Loosen shells from pans with a sharp knife. Remove from pans; let cool completely on wire racks. Yield: 20 shells.

◆

Scrumptious Endings

Toffee
Cream Torte

♦

6 (1.4-ounce) English
   toffee-flavored candy
   bars, coarsely chopped
   and divided

1 quart coffee ice cream,
   softened

2 tablespoons dark rum

1 (10¾-ounce) loaf frozen
   pound cake, thawed

4 ounces bittersweet
   chocolate, chopped

½ cup slivered almonds,
   toasted

1 quart chocolate ice
   cream, softened

2 tablespoons Barnie's
   Irish Cream Flavoring
   Syrup or crème de cacao

♦

Sprinkle half of chopped candy bars in an ungreased 10-inch springform pan; reserve remaining half for topping.

Combine coffee ice cream and rum; spread over candy bar layer in pan. Cover and freeze until firm.

Cut pound cake into ½-inch slices. Arrange cake slices over frozen ice cream layer; cover and freeze until firm.

Place chocolate in top of a double boiler; bring water to a boil. Reduce heat to low; cook until chocolate melts, stirring occasionally. Remove from heat, and stir in almonds. Spread mixture over frozen pound cake layer; cover and freeze until firm.

Combine chocolate ice cream and flavoring syrup; spread over frozen chocolate layer. Sprinkle with half of reserved chopped candy bars; cover and freeze until firm.

Let stand at room temperature 5 minutes before serving. Carefully remove sides of springform pan. Gently press remaining chopped candy bars into sides of torte. Serve immediately. Yield: 10 to 12 servings.

Banana

Banshee Cappuccino

Pour cold milk into a chilled steaming pitcher. Steam and froth milk to 155°. Pour espresso and flavoring syrup into a large coffee cup or mug. Stir well. Fill with steamed milk. Spoon a 2-inch "cap" of foamed milk on top. Sprinkle with Sweet Vanilla Cappuccino Cappers. Serve immediately. Yield: 1 (1½-cup) serving.

◆

½ cup milk

¼ cup plus 2 tablespoons freshly brewed espresso (2 shots)

2 tablespoons Barnie's Banana Flavoring Syrup

Barnie's Sweet Vanilla Cappuccino Cappers®

Black Forest

Mocha Cooler

Combine first 4 ingredients in a beverage shaker. Add 1 cup small ice cubes. Cover and shake vigorously. Pour into tall glasses. Top each with whipped cream and a cherry. Yield: 2 (1½-cup) servings.

◆

1 cup milk

1 cup Barnie's Decadent Dark Chocolate Coffee Cooler®

¼ cup chocolate syrup

1 tablespoon Barnie's Cherry Flavoring Syrup

Sweetened whipped cream

Maraschino cherries

◆

Razzle Dazzle

Frappé

2 cups ice cubes

¼ cup half-and-half

3 to 4 tablespoons cold
brewed espresso (1 shot)

2 tablespoons Barnie's
Cherry Flavoring Syrup

1 tablespoon Barnie's
Almond Flavoring Syrup

Garnishes: maraschino
cherries, toasted slivered
almonds

Combine first 5 ingredients in container of an electric blender; cover and process 30 seconds or just until smooth. Pour into a tall glass. Garnish, if desired. Serve immediately. Yield: 1 (2-cup) serving.

Frappé is a slushy beverage that can easily be served as a refreshing icy dessert.

Neapolitan
Freeze

Combine all ingredients in container of an electric blender; cover and process 20 seconds or just until blended. Pour into glasses, and serve immediately. Yield: 2 (1½-cup) servings.

◆

2½ cups vanilla ice cream

½ cup milk

¼ cup Barnie's Decadent Dark Chocolate Coffee Cooler®

¼ cup Barnie's Vanilla Cream Coffee Cooler®

¼ cup Barnie's Strawberry Flavoring Syrup

Toasted Almond
Freeze

Combine first 5 ingredients in container of an electric blender; cover and process just until smooth and blended. Pour into a tall glass. Top with whipped cream. Serve immediately. Yield: 1 (1½-cup) serving.

◆

1 cup ice cubes

½ cup vanilla ice cream

⅓ cup Barnie's Latte Coffee Cooler®

3 tablespoons amaretto

1 tablespoon Barnie's Almond Flavoring Syrup

Sweetened whipped cream

Banana Split
Shake

1 cup ice cubes

1 cup Barnie's Vanilla
  Cream Coffee Cooler®

½ cup milk

¼ cup Barnie's Caramel
  Flavoring Syrup

2 tablespoons chocolate
  syrup

½ large ripe banana

  Sweetened whipped
  cream

  Chopped pecans

  Chopped maraschino
  cherries

  Garnish: banana slices

Combine first 6 ingredients in container of an electric blender; cover and process until smooth, stopping once to scrape down sides. Pour into glasses. Top with whipped cream, pecans, and cherries. Garnish, if desired. Serve immediately. Yield: 2 (1⅔-cup) servings.

For an even thicker, frostier shake, freeze the banana before adding it to the blender.

The Scottish philosopher Sir James MacKintosh (1765-1832) proposed that "the powers of a man's mind are directly proportional to the quantity of coffee he drank."

Blackberry
Cobbler Latte

½ cup milk

1½ teaspoons Barnie's
Blackberry Flavoring
Syrup

3 to 4 tablespoons freshly
brewed espresso (1 shot)

1 tablespoon Barnie's
Caramel Flavoring
Syrup

Pour cold milk and Blackberry Flavoring
Syrup into a chilled steaming pitcher. Steam
milk mixture to 155°. Pour milk mixture into
an 8-ounce cup or glass. Combine espresso
and Caramel Flavoring Syrup; stir well. Pour
espresso mixture over steamed milk. Serve
immediately. Yield: 1 (1-cup) serving.

Café
Caribbean

2 tablespoons Tia Maria or
other coffee-flavored
liqueur

2 tablespoons dark rum

¼ cup freshly brewed
espresso (1 shot)

½ cup hot water

Sweetened whipped
cream

Pour Tia Maria and rum into a 10-ounce
mug; add espresso and hot water. Stir well.
Top with whipped cream. Yield: 1 (1-cup)
serving.

(Photograph of Café Caribbean on page 79)

Café
Viennese

Pour Kahlúa and crème de cacao into a 10-ounce mug; add espresso and hot water. Stir well. Top with whipped cream. Yield: 1 (1-cup) serving.

◆

2 tablespoons Kahlúa or other coffee-flavored liqueur

2 tablespoons crème de cacao

¼ cup freshly brewed espresso (1 shot)

½ cup hot water

Sweetened whipped cream

◆

Rocky
Road

Pour Frangelico and crème de cacao into a 10-ounce mug; add espresso and hot chocolate. Stir well. Top with marshmallows. Serve immediately. Yield: 1 (1-cup) serving.

2 tablespoons Frangelico

2 tablespoons crème de cacao

¼ cup freshly brewed espresso (1 shot)

½ cup hot chocolate

Miniature marshmallows

◆

Velvet

Hammer

◆

½ cup plus 1 tablespoon
Irish cream liqueur

⅓ cup vodka

3 tablespoons amaretto

3 to 4 tablespoons freshly
brewed espresso (1 shot)

Sweetened whipped cream

Pour first 3 ingredients into a 12-ounce mug;
add espresso. Stir well. Top with whipped
cream. Serve immediately. Yield: 1 (1¼-cup)
serving.

◆

1½ tablespoons Barnie's
Caramel Flavoring
Syrup

2 teaspoons chocolate
syrup

¼ cup milk

3 to 4 tablespoons freshly
brewed espresso (1 shot)

Sweetened whipped cream

Caramel topping

Caramel Nut

Mocha

Pour syrups into an 8-ounce cup or glass. Pour
cold milk into a chilled steaming pitcher. Steam
milk to 155°. Add espresso to cup; stir well.
Fill cup with steamed milk. Top with whipped
cream. Drizzle caramel topping over whipped
cream. Serve immediately. Yield: 1 (1-cup)
serving.

(Photograph of Caramel Nut Mocha on page 64)

◆

Scrumptious Endings

Cherry

Macaroon Mocha

Pour syrups and amaretto into a 12-ounce cup or glass. Pour cold milk into a chilled steaming pitcher. Steam milk to 155°. Add espresso to cup; stir well. Fill cup with steamed milk. Top with Sweet Vanilla Cappuccino Cappers. Serve immediately. Yield: 1 (1½-cup) serving.

◆

2 tablespoons Barnie's Cherry Flavoring Syrup

2 tablespoons chocolate syrup

2 tablespoons amaretto

½ cup milk

¼ cup plus 2 tablespoons freshly brewed espresso

Barnie's Sweet Vanilla Cappuccino Cappers®

Hazelnut

Truffle Mocha

Pour syrups into a 12-ounce cup or glass. Pour cold milk into a chilled steaming pitcher. Steam milk to 155°. Add espresso to cup; stir well. Fill cup with steamed milk. Serve immediately. Yield: 1 (1-cup) serving.

◆

1 tablespoon chocolate syrup

1 tablespoon Barnie's Hazelnut Flavoring Syrup

¼ cup milk

¼ cup freshly brewed espresso (1 shot)

◆

COFFEE GLOSSARY

Acidity: A bright taste found in the body of a good cup of coffee or espresso.

Americano: A coffee beverage made by adding 2 parts hot water to 1 part espresso.

Arabica: *Coffea arabica* is the original species of the coffee plant found growing wild in Ethiopia, Africa. Arabica beans are the most sought-after coffee beans in the world due to their intense flavor.

Aroma: The delightful bouquet of aromatic gases released by freshly ground and brewed coffee.

Bitter: A taste perceived on the back of the tongue. A slightly bittersweet flavor in dark roasts is a desired characteristic.

Blend: A marriage of two or more coffee bean varieties to produce an overall balance and complexity that straight origin coffees rarely match.

Body: The strength and viscosity of a coffee extraction such as light, medium, full, or heavy.

Breve: Made like a latte except it combines espresso with steamed half-and-half instead of milk.

Café au Lait: The French way of enjoying coffee, using equal parts of regular brewed coffee and steamed milk poured simultaneously into a large cup.

Café con Leche: The Spanish version of a latte, using one-third espresso and two-thirds slightly frothed milk.

Caffè Latte: A popular morning coffee drink containing one-third espresso with two-thirds steamed milk and topped with little or no froth.

Cappuccino: One-third espresso capped with one-third steamed milk and one-third foamed milk. The drink gets its name from the foam "cap," which is said to resemble the Catholic order of Capuchin friars' hooded robes.

Crema: The rich and aromatic golden foam (cream) that tops a perfect cup of espresso.

Demitasse: French for "half-cup." The small cups in which espresso is traditionally served.

Espresso: An intensely rich coffee beverage made by rapidly forcing water and steam under pressure through finely ground, dark roasted coffee beans in an espresso machine.

Flavor: Describes the tastes and aromas given by the coffee; its total balance of body, aroma, and acidity.

Mocha: A latte made with chocolate syrup and topped with steamed milk.

Varietal Coffees: Unblended, straight coffees from a specific country or region.

RECIPE INDEX